SENSATIONAL DESIGNS USING COLOR,
VALUE & GEOMETRIC SHAPES · 12 PROJECTS

3-D Illusion Quilts
simplified

RUTH ANN BERRY

C&T PUBLISHING
Another Maker Inspired!

Text and photography copyright © 2024 by Ruth Ann Berry

Artwork copyright © 2024 by C&T Publishing, Inc.

Publisher: Amy Barrett-Daffin

Creative Director: Gailen Runge

Senior Editor: Roxane Cerda

Editor: Gailen Runge

Technical Editor: Debbie Rodgers

Cover/Book Designer: April Mostek

Production Coordinator: Zinnia Heinzmann

Illustrator: Kirstie L. Pettersen

Photography Coordinator: Rachel Ackley

Photography by Twinlight Studios unless otherwise noted

Published by C&T Publishing, Inc., P.O. Box 1456, Lafayette, CA 94549

Library of Congress Cataloging-in-Publication Data

Names: Berry, Ruth Ann, 1960- author.

Title: 3-D illusion quilts simplified : sensational designs using color, value & geometric shapes; 12 projects / Ruth Ann Berry.

Description: Lafayette, CA : C&T Publishing, [2024] | Summary: "Included inside for readers are twelve projects that vary in size and style from a wall hanging to a king-size quilt and medallion-style designs and continuous/repeating patterns, a section on designing their own 3-D quilts with isometric graph paper to use to sketch their own quilts, and more"-- Provided by publisher.

Identifiers: LCCN 2024004638 | ISBN 9781644035184 (trade paperback) | ISBN 9781644035191 (ebook)

Subjects: LCSH: Quilting. | Quilting--Patterns. | BISAC: CRAFTS & HOBBIES / Quilts & Quilting | CRAFTS & HOBBIES / Sewing

Classification: LCC TT835 .B4274 2024 | DDC 746.46--dc23/eng/20240310

LC record available at https://lccn.loc.gov/2024004638

Printed in China

10 9 8 7 6 5 4 3 2 1

Dedication

I would like to dedicate this book to my friend Jane, who I would love to claim as my best friend. However, I think I would have to stand in line. So many people are blessed by her friendship that I would have stiff competition vying for position as "bestie." Her steadfast encouragement and support have been one of the best things to happen in my quilting and life journey.

Acknowledgments

Stitch Master and business partner Greg Barner has once again accomplished most of the sewing work for this book. His vision, encouragement, and "quality nagging" are the moxie that turn ideas into quilts.

Contents

PROJECTS 16

Escalator   34

Hygge   39

Whale's Tail   44

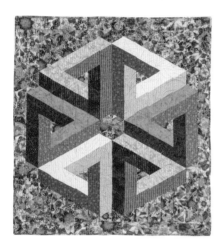

Huckleberry   48

Shenanigans   52

Limerick   56

Arpeggio   61

Better Together Bed Runner   66

introduction

Optical illusion art is my favorite drawing style. I love studying the shading and shaping that causes a drawing on a flat surface to appear dimensional. If the shading and shaping can be rendered in fabric, all the better. Isometric graph paper allows anything drawn on it to become a 3-D quilt by simply constructing the rows of 60° triangles. That makes it the perfect medium for someone who loves to draw and also loves quilting.

Making a 3-D Quilt

Tools

You won't need any specialized tools for these 3-D quilts, just a 60° triangle ruler and other basic sewing supplies. Here's a list of the tools I used.

- Rotary cutter and mat
- 6˝ × 24˝ straight ruler
- 60° Triangle Ruler with one blunt point
- Scissors
- Pins
- Marking pencil
- Clothes pins or binder clips

60° RULER OPTIONS

You don't have to buy a new 60° triangle ruler if yours doesn't have a blunt tip. To use a ruler with a pointed tip, align the bottom of the fabric strip with the ruler mark that is ¼˝ more than the width of the strip.

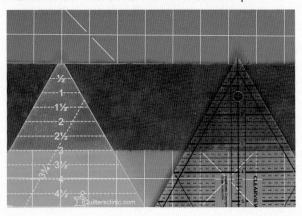

Selecting Fabric

For your 3-D quilt, choose blender, solid, or tone-on-tone fabrics in sets of three. Each box, beam, or square-nut element requires three fabrics—a light, a medium, and a dark. One option is to select fabrics of the same color in three values, as in *Gnarly* (page 17). The fabrics within each colorway should graduate smoothly from light to dark but have enough contrast to be easily differentiated from each other.

Another option is to choose three different colors for an element, still using a light, medium, and dark value but not necessarily the same color, as in *Limerick* (page 56).

Using the Project Page

Each project page features a cutting chart in table form that contains each fabric's color description, yardage requirement, the number of strips to cut across the width of the fabric, and the number of triangles to cut from the strips.

Color	Yardage	Strips to cut	Triangles to cut from strips

Each of the projects offers two finished-size options based on the cut width of the strips or the portion of the chart used. The strip width and finished size information is located at the top of the cutting chart. The yardage requirements and cutting instructions are provided for both size options. The patterns are easily sized up and down by changing the width of the strips. The continuous pattern projects, *Lattices* (page 25) and *Escalator* (page 34), can be made using the full chart for the larger-size quilt or the red-outlined portion of the chart for the smaller-size quilt.

Making the Quilt

CUTTING TRIANGLES FROM STRIPS

1. From the project page, choose a finished size and note the width of the strips required.

2. Cut the required number of width-of-fabric strips as indicated in the chart.

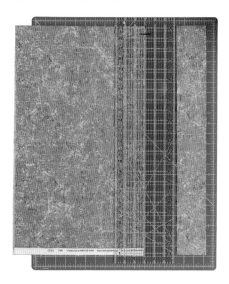

3. Starting at the selvage end of the strips, use a blunt-pointed 60° ruler to subcut the strips into equilateral triangles. *Note: Do not cut the border fabric into triangles!* If you have a 60° ruler with a pointed tip, see 60° Ruler Options (page 7).

> **TIP** How Many Triangles Can You Get From a Strip?

Assuming your fabric has 40˝ of usable width, you should be able to cut the following 60° triangles from one strip:

- 2½˝ strip: 21 triangles
- 3˝ strip: 18 triangles
- 3½˝ strip: 15 triangles
- 4˝ strip: 13 triangles

STACKING IN COLUMNS

1. Referring to the design chart, stack the triangles needed for each column in order from top to bottom, with the first triangle for the top of the column on top of the stack.

2. Clip each stacked column together using a large project clip or clothespin.

Optional: Alternatively, you may choose to keep each color stacked separately and add triangles one at a time as you sew, marking off the design chart as you go.

SEWING COLUMNS

1. Sew each column, working from top to bottom. Match the orientation of each triangle to the design chart. Use the blunt point as a "direction indicator" and alternate the right/left orientation of each new triangle. You can chain piece the triangles in pairs, then sets of 4, then sets of 8, and so on. Or if you find that confusing, you can also just add triangles one at a time working down the column. **A**

2. If you are chain piecing, work down the column, sewing triangles together in pairs. Lay the first triangle in each pair on top of the next triangle, right sides together. Match the pointed tips. Using a ¼˝ seam allowance, sew the seam along the edge opposite the pointed tips. **B**

3. Press all of the seams between triangles open. Don't trim off the "tails" **C**

4. When chain piecing, sew the pairs into sets of 4, then sets of 8, and so on. **D**

5. Use the pressed out "tails" to line up the pairs. **E**

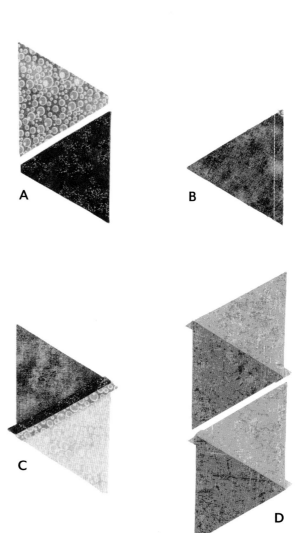

JOINING COLUMNS TOGETHER

Attach the rows together, working from left to right across the design chart. Use the pressed-out points to match each row to the next.

TIP ▶ **Alternate Sewing Direction**

To avoid a curved result, alternate sewing direction with each new column, stitching from top to bottom, then bottom to top.

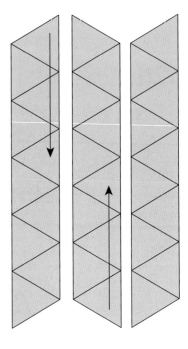

TRIMMING TO SQUARE

Trim the top and bottom edges of the quilt to square. Leave ¼" seam allowance.

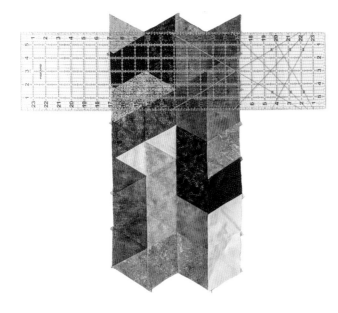

ADDING BORDERS

I usually add a simple border in the same fabric and strip width as the background fabric. This gives the design the appearance of "floating" on the background. I have listed the border yardage requirements separately from the background in the project charts so you can choose whatever fabric you wish. To add borders, measure the length of the side of the quilt to be bordered. Cut and piece a border strip to that length. Match the center of the border strip to the center of the quilt edge and pin in place. Pin the border to the quilt edge, working from the center outward in both directions. Stitch in place.

FINISHING

Finish and bind using your preferred technique. Each project includes the yardage amounts that allow for 2½"-wide binding strips.

Alternative Construction Options

Many people have asked about using long strips with ends cut at 60° angles to avoid sewing so many identical triangles. Overall, it may be easier to match up the columns by constructing all of them with triangles, but if you would like to cut fewer triangles and sew fewer seams, and are confident in your measuring and ¼"-seam skills, here's how that can work for you.

BACKGROUND STRIPS THAT "RUN OFF" THE TOP AND BOTTOM OF THE QUILT

For a drawing containing columns that start and end with many background triangles, a single long strip with one end cut at a 60° angle can be used in place of the triangle sections that "run off" the top and bottom of the quilt. The strips can be left longer than necessary and trimmed to square once the quilt top construction is complete.

Hygge (page 39) contains a chart with the top and bottom calculations already completed. The tops and bottoms of the columns may not match exactly when sewing the columns together. Instead, match the triangles within the columns to the preceding columns as shown in the design chart, and leave the tops and bottoms long and uneven for trimming and bordering later.

INTERNAL PIECES

Triangle sections that are "internal," meaning they are in the center of the drawing, can also be replaced with single longer pieces. The chart on page 12 contains the measurements for 2 to 21 triangle replacement pieces for the various widths of strips. The measurement listed is the length of the rectangle that you would need to cut from the strip. You would then need to cut the rectangle's ends at a 60° angle to match the shape of the piece in the chart.

Lattices (page 25) contains alternate cutting and sewing instructions with the cut lengths of the replacement pieces provided for columns 1 and 2.

Trim the cut rectangle ends to match the triangles it is replacing. In the projects they are noted as follows:

right/left: The top triangle points to the right and the bottom triangle points to the left.

left/right: The top triangle points to the left and the bottom triangle points to the right.

right/right: Both the top and bottom triangles point to the right.

left/left: Both the top and bottom triangles point to the left.

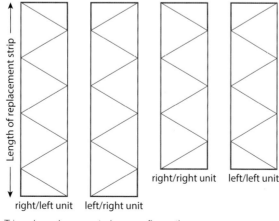

Triangle replacement piece configurations

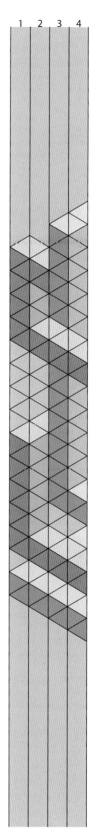

First 4 columns of *Hygge* with background strips.

Use the chart below to calculate the vertical *cut* length of the replacement strip, based on the number of triangles you are replacing and the width of the strip. Once you cut your strip, cut the ends to match the triangles it is replacing, following instructions on page 11.

TRIANGLE REPLACEMENT CHART				
Number of triangles to replace	**Width of strips**			
	2½″	3″	3½″	4″
2	4⅜″	5¼″	6″	6⅞″
3	5½″	6⅝″	7¾″	9″
4	6⅝″	8⅛″	9½″	11″
5	7¾″	9½″	11¼″	13″
6	9″	11″	13″	15″
7	10⅛″	12⅜″	14¾″	17″
8	11¼″	13⅞″	16⅜″	19″
9	12⅜″	15⅜″	18⅛″	21⅛″
10	13⅝″	16¾″	19⅞″	23⅛″
11	14¾″	18¼″	21⅝″	25⅛″
12	15⅞″	19⅝″	23⅜″	27⅛″
13	17″	21⅛″	25⅛″	28⅛″
14	18¼″	22½″	26⅞″	31⅛″
15	19⅜″	24″	28½″	33⅛″
16	20½″	25⅜″	30¼″	35¼″
17	21⅝″	26⅞″	32″	37¼″
18	22¾″	28⅜″	33¾″	39¼″
19	24″	29¾″	35½″	41¼″
20	25⅛″	31¼″	37¼″	43¼″
21	26¼″	32⅝″	38⅞″	45¼″

Designing Your Own 3-D Elements

Overview

I draw everything on isometric graph paper, visualizing an imaginary light source in the upper right-hand corner of the page. That means that the lightest value is usually on the top of the drawing, the darkest value faces bottom left, and the medium value faces bottom right.

Use the isometric graph paper on pages 69–78 to design your own 3-D elements.

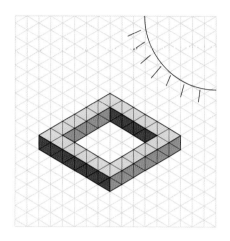
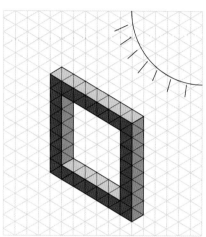

Drawing Horizontal Diamonds

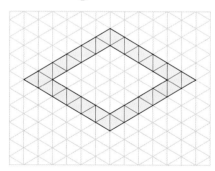

1. Draw a 12-block horizontal diamond.

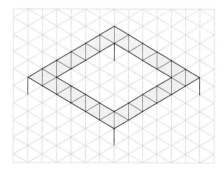

2. Draw vertical lines one block down from all of the corners.

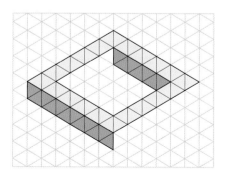
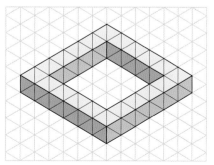

3. Add 60° lines and shading parallel to the original diamond lines.

Drawing Left- and Right-Facing Vertical Diamonds

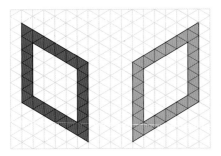 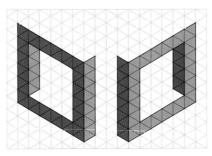 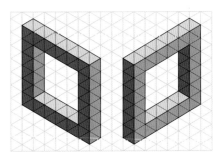

1. Draw 12-block vertical diamonds.

2. Draw 60° lines one block to the right from all corners for the left-facing diamond and one block to the left from all the corners for the right-facing diamond.

3. Add a second set of lines parallel and shading to the original diamond lines.

Linking Diamonds

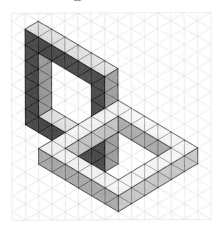 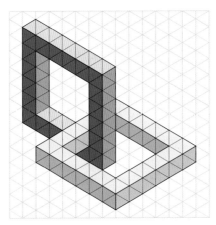

1. To link two diamonds, draw complete horizontal and vertical diamonds next to each other.

2. Erase the lines you would like to have appear behind.

Drawing Crisscrossing 3-D Beams

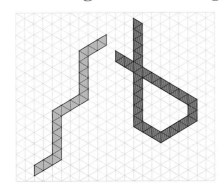 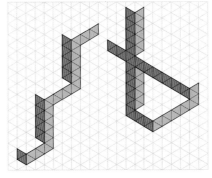 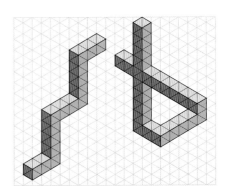

1. Begin by drawing the outline of a beam that moves in a zig zag or loop-de-loop on the page.

2. Add parallel lines for dimension.

3. Erase the lines that you want to appear behind.

Drawing Simple Shapes on Isometric Paper; Hearts and Stars

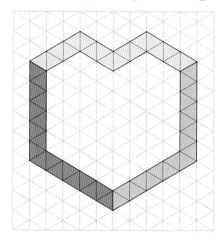 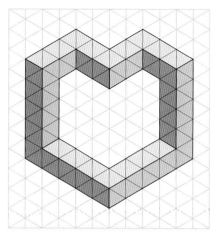

1. Any recognizable motif that can be approximated with 60° angles can be made to appear 3-D by first drawing the shape, then adding parallel lines.

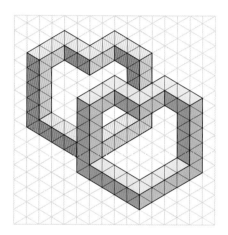 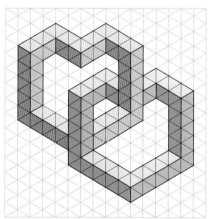

2. Objects can be linked by drawing them next to each other, then erasing the lines you would like to have appear behind.

Drawing "Impossible" Triangles

An "impossible triangle" is essentially three number 7's, a light, a medium and a dark.

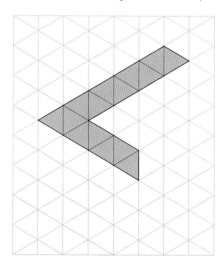 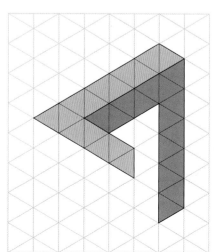 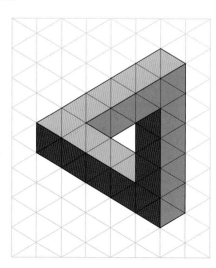

PROJECTS

Gnarly

Finished quilt sizes:
63″ × 79″ and 88″ × 110½″

Gnarly evolved from an earlier drawing that I thought could benefit from more 3-D elements and less background. I was pleased with the results so I gave it a name whose slang meaning still transmits a positive idea that describes something awesome, cool, or excellent.

Draw It

Refer to Drawing Left- and Right-Facing Vertical Diamonds (page 14) to see the building blocks for the *Gnarly* drawing.

1. Draw 3 sets of 12-block right-facing diamonds. **A**

2. Add 2 sets of left-facing diamonds. The center 2 are 8-block diamonds, and the outer 2 are 12-block diamonds. **B**

3. Add 2 more 12-block left-facing diamonds. **C**

A

B

C

Materials and Cutting

Start by cutting the number of strips in the width required for your quilt, then cut the strips into triangles (page 8).

	YARDAGE REQUIREMENTS, WIDTH OF STRIPS, NUMBER OF STRIPS TO CUT					
Fabrics	**63″ × 79″ Quilt: Cut 3″ Strips**		**88″ × 110½″ Quilt: Cut 4″ Strips**		**Triangles to cut from strips**	
	Yardage	**3″ Strips to Cut**	**Yardage**	**4″ Strips to Cut**		
Light Blue	⅓ yard	3	⅝ yard	4	47	
Medium Blue	⅓ yard	3	⅝ yard	4	48	
Dark Blue	⅔ yard	6	1 yard	7	97	
Light Red	¼ yard	2	½ yard	3	31	
Medium Red	½ yard	4	¾ yard	5	68	
Dark Red	¼ yard	2	½ yard	3	35	
Light Yellow	¼ yard	2	⅓ yard	2	23	
Medium Yellow	¼ yard	2	½ yard	3	31	
Dark Yellow	½ yard	4	⅔ yard	5	56	
Light Green	⅓ yard	3	⅝ yard	4	49	
Medium Green	⅝ yard	6	1 yard	7	95	
Dark Green	⅓ yard	3	½ yard	4	45	
Light Purple	¼ yard	2	⅓ yard	2	27	
Medium Purple	½ yard	4	⅔ yard	5	61	
Dark Purple	¼ yard	2	½ yard	3	34	
Background	2¼ yards	25	4¼ yards	35	449	
Border	¾ yard	8	1¼ yards	11		
Backing	5 yards		8 yards			
Binding	⅝ yard		⅞ yard			
Batting	71″ × 87″		96″ × 119″			

Construction

See Making a 3-D Quilt (page 7) for complete instructions on sewing the columns of triangles and assembling the quilt.

SEW THE COLUMNS

1. For column 1, start with a background triangle with the blunt point oriented towards the left, then add the next background triangle with the blunt point facing the right.

To continue the first column, *add triangles in this order:*

20 more background triangles

1 light red

12 dark red

17 background

2. For column 2, start with a background triangle with the blunt point oriented towards the right, then add the next background triangle with the blunt point facing left.

To continue the second column, *add triangles in this order:*

19 more background triangles

2 light red

12 medium red

17 background

3. Follow the *Gnarly* design chart (page 20) and continue to build columns 3–23 in the same manner.

QUILT ASSEMBLY

1. Sew the columns together.

2. Trim the top and bottom of the quilt to square as described in Trimming to Square (page 10).

BORDERS

See Adding Borders (page 10). Before you cut the borders, measure your pieced quilt top and adjust the following sizes to match your quilt.

1. For the 63˝ × 79˝ quilt, make 2 side borders 3˝ × 74¼˝ and 2 top and bottoms borders 3˝ × 63˝.

For the 88˝ × 110½˝ quilt, make 2 side borders 4˝ × 103½˝ and 2 top and bottom borders 4˝ × 88˝.

2. Add the side borders to the quilt, then add the top and bottom borders.

alternate color inspiration

Gnarly Design Chart

Night Song

Night Song was an experiment in making a recognizable motif into a 3-D object, then linking a group of them. The challenge was to decide which lines should be hidden and which would show in the foreground.

Draw It

Refer to Designing Your Own 3-D Elements (page 15) to see the building blocks for the *Night Song* drawing.

1. Draw a single 3-D star. **A**

2. Add a second star over the top of the first, erasing the part of the first star to appear behind. **B**

3. Add a third star over the top of the first 2, erasing the lines of the first two stars to appear behind. **C**

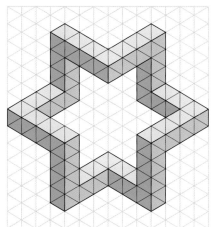

A

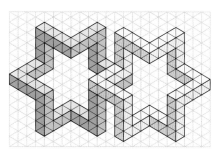

B

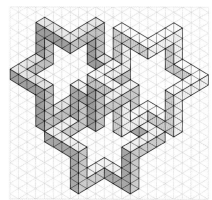

C

Materials and Cutting

Start by cutting the number of strips in the width required for your quilt, then cut the strips into triangles (page 8).

	YARDAGE REQUIREMENTS, WIDTH OF STRIPS, NUMBER OF STRIPS TO CUT				
Fabrics	**58½″ × 76″ Quilt: cut 2½″ strips**		**73″ × 95″ Quilt: Cut 3″ strips**		**Triangles to cut from strips**
	Yardage	**2½″ strips to cut**	**Yardage**	**3″ strips to cut**	
Light Green	⅓ yard	4	½ yard	4	66
Medium Green	⅓ yard	4	½ yard	5	76
Dark Green	⅓ yard	4	½ yard	5	79
Light Yellow	⅓ yard	4	½ yard	4	72
Medium Yellow	⅓ yard	4	½ yard	5	80
Dark Yellow	⅓ yard	4	½ yard	5	74
Light Aqua	⅓ yard	4	½ yard	4	70
Medium Aqua	⅓ yard	4	½ yard	5	74
Dark Aqua	⅓ yard	4	½ yard	5	74
Light Purple	⅓ yard	4	½ yard	4	68
Medium Purple	⅓ yard	4	½ yard	5	76
Dark Purple	⅓ yard	4	½ yard	5	84
Background	3 yards	39	4 yards	45	808
Border	⅝ yard	7	⅞ yard	9	
Backing	4¾ yards		6¾ yards		
Binding	⅝ yard		⅞ yard		
Batting	67″ × 84″		81″ × 103″		

Construction

See Making a 3-D Quilt (page 7) for complete instructions on sewing the columns of triangles and assembling the quilt.

SEW THE COLUMNS

1. For column 1, start with a background triangle with the blunt point oriented towards the left, then add the next background triangle with the blunt point facing to the right.

To continue the first column, *add triangles in this order:*

  10 more background triangles

  1 light green

  2 dark green

  21 background

  1 light purple

  2 dark purple

  24 background

2. For column 2, start with a background triangle with the blunt point oriented towards the right, then add the next background triangle with the blunt point facing to the left.

To continue the second column, *add triangles in this order:*

  9 more background triangles

  3 light green

  2 dark green

  19 background

  3 light purple

  2 dark purple

  23 background

3. Follow the *Night Song* design chart (page 24) and continue to build columns 3–27 in the same manner.

QUILT ASSEMBLY

1. Sew the columns together.

2. Trim the top and bottom of the quilt to square as described in Trimming to Square (page 10).

BORDERS

See Adding Borders (page 10). Before you cut the borders, measure your pieced quilt top and adjust the following sizes to match your quilt.

1. For the 58½˝ × 76˝ quilt, make 2 side borders 2½˝ × 72˝ and top and bottom borders 2½˝ × 58½˝.

For the 73˝ × 95˝ quilt, make 2 side borders 3˝ × 90˝ and top and bottom borders 3˝ × 73˝.

2. Add the side borders to the quilt, then add the top and bottom borders.

alternate color inspiration

Night Song Design Chart

Lattices

Finished quilt sizes:
40½˝ × 64˝ and 70½˝ × 93˝

The *Lattices* drawing evolved from a Rideshare carpool sign I saw along the highway on one of our trips to a quilt show.

Draw It

Refer to Drawing Crisscrossing 3-D Beams (page 14) to see the building blocks for the *Lattices* drawing.

1. Draw 2 criss-crossing beams from upper right to lower left. **A**

2. Draw a second pair of beams alongside the first set. **B**

3. Continue to add pairs of beams to the right margin, then add beam pairs from right to left to the left margin. **C**

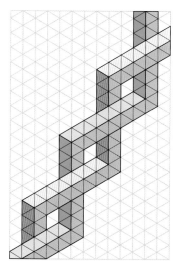

A

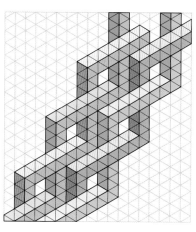

B

C

Materials and Cutting

Start by cutting the number of strips in the width required for your quilt, then cut the strips into triangles (page 8).

	YARDAGE REQUIREMENTS, WIDTH OF STRIPS, NUMBER OF STRIPS TO CUT					
Fabrics	**40½″ × 64″ quilt, cut 3″ strips**			**70½″ × 93″ quilt, cut 3″ strips**		
	Yardage	**3″ strips to cut**	**Triangles to cut**	**Yardage**	**3″ Strips to cut**	**Triangles to cut from strips**
Light Purple	½ yard	4	56	¾ yard	8	130
Medium Purple	⅝ yard	6	92	1¼ yards	13	217
Dark Purple	⅓ yard	3	37	½ yard	5	89
Light Brown	½ yard	4	60	¾ yard	8	132
Medium Brown	⅝ yard	6	98	1⅛ yards	12	215
Dark Brown	⅓ yard	3	39	½ yard	5	83
Light Orange	⅓ yard	3	44	¾ yard	8	132
Medium Orange	½ yard	5	79	1⅛ yards	12	212
Dark Orange	¼ yard	2	36	½ yard	5	89
Light Teal	⅓ yard	3	43	¾ yard	8	133
Medium Teal	½ yard	4	69	1⅛ yards	12	216
Dark Teal	¼ yard	2	30	½ yard	5	86
Black	¼ yard	2	37	½ yard	5	86
Backing	2¾ yards			6⅝ yards		
Binding	½ yard			¾ yard		
Batting	49″ × 72″			79″ × 101″		

Construction

See Making a 3-D Quilt (page 7) for complete instructions on sewing the columns of triangles and assembling the quilt.

Note: For the 40½˝ × 63½˝ quilt, make only the red outlined portion of the design chart (page 29). For the 70½˝ × 93˝ quilt, use the whole chart.

SEW THE COLUMNS

1. For column 1, start with a medium teal triangle with the blunt point oriented towards the right, then add a black triangle with the blunt point facing to the left.

To continue the first column, *add triangles in this order:*

1 black triangle	6 medium purple
2 light purple	2 light brown
2 medium purple	2 medium brown
1 light brown	2 black (end of smaller quilt)
5 dark brown	
2 light orange	2 light orange
2 medium orange	2 medium orange
3 dark brown	1 light teal
1 light brown	5 dark teal
2 medium brown	2 light purple
2 light purple	2 medium purple
4 medium purple	3 dark teal
2 light teal	1 light teal
2 medium teal	2 medium teal

2. For column 2, start with a dark purple triangle with the blunt point oriented towards the left, then add the next dark purple triangle with the blunt point facing to the right.

To continue the second column, *add triangles in this order:*

1 dark purple triangle	5 dark orange
1 light purple	2 light brown
2 medium purple	2 medium brown
2 light brown	3 dark orange (end of smaller quilt)
4 medium brown	
2 light orange	1 light orange
2 medium orange	2 medium orange
6 medium brown	2 light teal
2 light purple	4 medium teal
2 medium purple	2 light purple
2 black	2 medium purple
2 light teal	6 light teal
2 medium teal	1 light orange
1 light orange	

3. Follow the *Lattices* design chart (page 29) and continue to build columns 3–16 or 3–28 in the same manner.

ALTERNATE CUTTING AND COLUMN ASSEMBLY OPTION

If you'd like, you can replace some of the identical individual triangles with longer strips. See Alternative Construction Options (page 11). The alternate pieces will need to be trimmed as noted to match the triangles they replace.

1. Start with a medium teal triangle with the blunt point oriented towards the right. *Add pieces in this order:*

1 black left/right piece cut at 5¼˝

1 light purple left/right piece cut 5¼˝

1 medium purple left/right piece cut 5¼˝

1 light brown triangle

1 dark brown right/right piece, cut 9½˝

1 light orange left/right piece cut 5¼˝

1 medium orange left/left piece cut 5¼˝

1 dark brown left/left piece cut 6⅝˝

1 light brown triangle

1 medium brown left/right piece cut 5¼˝

1 light purple left/right piece cut 5¼˝

1 medium purple left/right piece cut 8⅛˝

1 light teal left/right piece cut 5¼˝

1 medium teal left/right piece cut 5¼˝

1 medium purple left/right piece cut 11˝

1 light brown piece left/right cut 5¼˝

1 medium brown left/right piece cut 5¼˝

1 black left/right piece cut 5¼˝ (end of smaller quilt)

1 light orange left/right piece cut 5¼˝

1 medium orange left/right piece cut 5¼˝

1 light teal triangle

1 dark teal right/right piece cut 9½˝

1 light purple left/right piece cut 5¼˝

1 medium purple left/right piece cut 5¼˝

1 dark teal left/left piece cut 6⅝˝

1 light teal triangle

1 medium teal left/right piece cut 5¼˝

2. Continue to build columns 2–16 or 2–28 in the same manner, referring to the Triangle Replacement Chart (page 12) and the triangle replacement configuration illustration (page 11).

QUILT ASSEMBLY

1. Sew the columns together.

2. Trim the top and bottom of the quilt to square as described in Trimming to Square (page 10).

alternate color inspiration

1 2 3 4 5 6 7 8 9 10 11 12 13 14 15 16 17 18 19 20 21 22 23 24 25 26 27 28

Lattices Design Chart

Mango

Finished quilt sizes:
55½″ × 80½″ and 77½″ × 112½″

Mango gets its name from the "fruity" colors we used in it. We negotiated over a few other names like "Melon" and "Tangerine" but settled on the final name because it sounded more sophisticated.

Draw It

Refer to Drawing Crisscrossing 3-D Beams (page 14) to see the building blocks for the *Mango* drawing.

1. Start with an interlocking knot. **A**

2. Add a center connecting bow tie. **B**

3. Add a second interlocking knot upside down. **C**

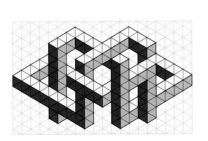

A

B

C

30

Materials and Cutting

Start by cutting the number of strips in the width required for your quilt, then cut the strips into triangles (page 8).

	YARDAGE REQUIREMENTS, WIDTH OF STRIPS, NUMBER OF STRIPS TO CUT				
Fabrics	55½˝ × 80½˝ quilt, cut 3˝ strips		77½˝ × 112½˝ quilt, cut 4˝ strips		**Triangles to cut from strips**
	Yardage	**3˝ strips to cut**	**Yardage**	**4˝ strips to cut**	
Yellow	1¼ yards	14	2¼ yards	19	236
Medium Orange	1¼ yards	13	2⅛ yards	18	228
Dark Orange	1¼ yards	14	2¼ yards	19	236
Background	1⅞ yards	20	3¼ yards	28	360
Border	⅔ yard	7	1⅓ yards	11	
Backing	5 yards		6¾ yards		
Binding	⅝ yard		⅞ yard		
Batting	64˝ × 89˝		86˝ × 121˝		

Construction

See Making a 3-D Quilt (page 7) for complete instructions on sewing the columns of triangles and assembling the quilt.

SEW THE COLUMNS

1. For column 1, start with a background triangle with the blunt point oriented towards the left, then add the next background triangle with the blunt point facing to the right.

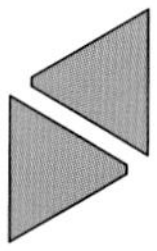

To continue the first column, *add triangles in this order:*

8 more background triangles

1 yellow

2 dark orange

3 background

1 yellow

9 dark orange

1 yellow

10 dark orange

3 background

1 yellow

2 dark orange

10 background

2. For column 2, start with a background triangle with the blunt point oriented towards the right, then add the next background triangle with the blunt point facing to the left.

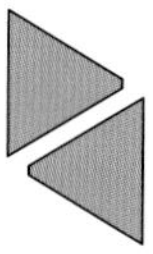

To continue the second column, *add triangles in this order:*

7 more background triangles

3 yellow

2 dark orange

2 background

2 yellow

2 dark orange

5 medium orange

2 yellow

10 medium orange

2 background

3 yellow

2 dark orange

9 background

3. Follow the *Mango* design chart (page 33) and continue to build columns 3–20 in the same manner.

QUILT ASSEMBLY

1. Sew the columns together.

2. Trim the top and bottom of the quilt to square as described in Trimming to Square (page 10).

BORDERS

See Adding Borders (page 10). Before you cut the borders, measure your pieced quilt top and adjust the following sizes to match your quilt.

1. For the 55½˝ × 80½˝ quilt, make 2 side borders 3˝ × 75½˝ and top and bottom borders 3˝ × 55½˝.

For the 77½˝ × 112½˝ quilt, make 2 side borders 4˝ × 105½˝ and top and bottom borders 4 × 77½˝.

2. Add the side borders to the quilt, then add the top and bottom borders.

alternate
color inspiration

1 2 3 4 5 6 7 8 9 10 11 12 13 14 15 16 17 18 19 20

Mango Design Chart

Escalator

Finished quilt sizes:
35½″ × 45″ and 65½″ × 85½″

The *Escalator* drawing gets its name from the uphill, then downhill look of the alternating "back leaning" and "forward leaning" diamonds.

Draw It

Refer to Drawing Horizontal Diamonds (page 13) to see the building blocks for the *Escalator* drawing.

1. Draw an 8-block tipped-back horizontal diamond. **A**

2. Stack a second 8-block diamond over the top of the first. Add a center post. **B**

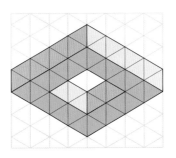

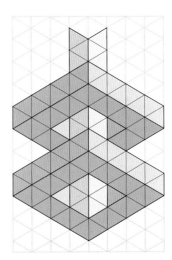

A   B

3. Draw an 8-block tipped-forward diamond. **C**

4. Stack a second 8-block diamond over the top of the first. Add a center post. **D**

5. Interlock alternating columns of tipped back and tipped forward diamonds with center posts. **E**

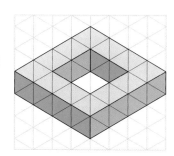

C

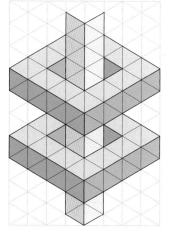

D

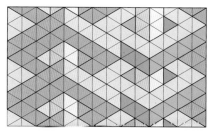

E

Materials and Cutting

Start by cutting the number of strips in the width required for your quilt, then cut the strips into triangles (page 8).

| Fabrics | YARDAGE REQUIREMENTS, WIDTH OF STRIPS, NUMBER OF STRIPS TO CUT | | | | | |
| | 35½˝ × 45˝ quilt, cut 3˝ strips | | | 65½˝ × 85½˝ quilt, cut 3˝ strips | | |
	Yardage	3˝ strips to cut	Triangles to cut	Yardage	3˝ strips to cut	Triangles to cut from strips
Light Blue	⅓ yard	3	47	1 yard	10	180
Medium Blue	½ yard	4	64	1⅛ yards	12	210
Dark Blue	⅝ yard	6	104	1⅔ yards	19	340
Light Green	⅔ yard	7	115	2 yards	23	410
Medium Green	⅓ yard	3	48	⅞ yard	9	160
Dark Green	¼ yard	2	28	⅝ yard	6	100
Light Gray	¼ yard	2	21	½ yard	5	80
Dark Gray	¼ yard	2	21	½ yard	5	80
Backing	2½ yards			5¼ yards		
Binding	½ yard			¾ yard		
Batting	44˝ × 53˝			74˝ × 94˝		

Construction

See Making a 3-D Quilt (page 7) for complete instructions on sewing the columns of triangles and assembling the quilt.

Note: For the 35½˝ × 45˝ quilt, make only the red outlined portion of the design chart (page 38). For the 65½˝ × 85½˝ quilt, use the whole chart.

SEW THE COLUMNS

1. For column 1, start with a dark blue triangle with the blunt point oriented towards the left, then add a light green triangle with the blunt point facing to the right.

2. For column 2, start with a dark blue triangle with the blunt point oriented towards the right, then add a dark blue triangle with the blunt point facing to the left.

To continue the first column, *add triangles in this order:*

2 light green triangles	3 light green (1 for smaller quilt)
2 medium blue	
1 dark blue	2 medium blue
3 light green	1 dark blue
2 medium blue	3 light green
1 dark blue	2 medium blue
3 light green	1 dark blue
2 medium blue	3 light green
1 dark blue	2 medium blue
3 light green	1 dark blue
2 medium blue	3 light green
1 dark blue	2 medium blue
3 light green	1 dark blue
2 medium blue	3 light green
1 dark blue	2 medium blue

To continue the second column, *add triangles in this order:*

1 light green	1 light green
2 medium blue	2 medium blue
3 dark blue	3 dark blue
1 light green	1 light green
2 medium blue	2 medium blue
3 dark blue	3 dark blue
1 light green	1 light green
2 medium blue	2 medium blue
3 dark blue	3 dark blue
1 light green	1 light green
2 medium blue	2 medium blue
3 dark blue	3 dark blue
1 light green	1 light green
2 medium blue	2 medium blue
3 dark blue (end for smaller quilt)	1 dark blue

3. Follow the *Escalator* design chart (page 38) and continue to build columns 3–14 or 3–26 in the same manner.

QUILT ASSEMBLY

1. Sew the columns together.

2. Trim the top and bottom of the quilt to square as described in Trimming to Square (page 10).

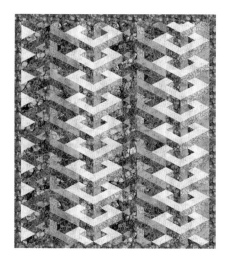

1 2 3 4 5 6 7 8 9 10 11 12 13 14 15 16 17 18 19 20 21 22 23 24 25 26

Escalator Design Chart

Hygge

Finished quilt sizes:
66½˝ × 84˝ and 83˝ × 105˝

From Wikipedia: "Hygge is a word in Danish and Norwegian that describes a mood of coziness and 'comfortable conviviality' with feelings of wellness and contentment." *Hygge* just seems like a perfect name for a quilt. Also, the blue and orange parts of the drawing are embracing each other in a hug.

Draw It

Refer to Drawing Crisscrossing 3-D Beams (page 14) to see the building blocks for the *Hygge* drawing.

1. Start with a continuous-line crisscrossing beam. **A**

2. Interlock a second continuous-line beam. **B**

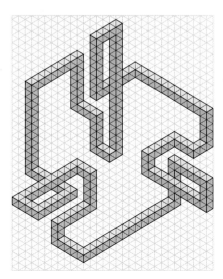

A

B

Materials and Cutting

Start by cutting the number of strips in the width required for your quilt, then cut the strips into triangles (page 8).

	YARDAGE REQUIREMENTS, WIDTH OF STRIPS, NUMBER OF STRIPS TO CUT				
Fabrics	66½″ × 84″ quilt, cut 2½″ strips		83″ × 105″ quilt, cut 3″ strips		**Triangles to cut from strips**
	Yardage	2½″ strips to cut	Yardage	3″ strips to cut	
Light Orange	¾ yard	9	1 yard	10	175
Medium Orange	⅞ yard	10	1 yard	11	196
Dark Orange	⅞ yard	10	1 yard	11	192
Light Blue	¾ yard	9	1 yard	10	173
Medium Blue	⅞ yard	10	1⅛ yards	12	200
Dark Blue	¾ yard	9	1 yard	11	187
Background	3⅝ yards	50	5⅛ yards	59	1047
Border	⅝ yard	8	1 yard	10	
Backing	5¼ yards		8 yards		
Binding	¾ yard		⅞ yard		
Batting	75″ × 92″		91″ × 113″		

Construction

See Making a 3-D Quilt (page 7) for complete instructions on sewing the columns of triangles and assembling the quilt.

SEW THE COLUMNS

1. For column 1, start with a background triangle with the blunt point oriented towards the right, then add the next background triangle with the blunt point facing to the left.

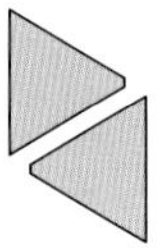

To continue the first column, *add triangles in this order:*

17 more background triangles	10 dark orange
1 light orange	1 background
8 dark orange	1 light blue
7 background	2 dark blue
1 light orange	20 background

2. For column 2, start with a background triangle with the blunt point oriented towards the left, then add the next background triangle with the blunt point facing to the right.

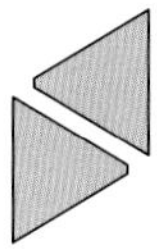

To continue the second column, *add triangles in this order:*

17 more background triangles	1 light orange	1 light orange
2 light orange	2 dark orange	2 dark orange
2 dark orange	5 background	2 light blue
3 medium orange	2 light orange	2 dark blue
	8 medium orange	19 background

3. Follow the *Hygge* design chart (page 43) and continue to build columns 3–31 in the same manner.

ALTERNATE CUTTING AND COLUMN ASSEMBLY OPTION

If you'd like, you can replace some of the sets of identical triangles that "run off" the top and bottom of the chart with longer strips. See Alternative Construction Options (page 11). The alternate pieces will need to be trimmed as noted to match the triangles they replace.

HYGGE ALTERNATE: LENGTH OF TOP AND BOTTOM STRIPS IN INCHES FOR THE 83″ × 105″ QUILT											
Column #	1	2	3	4	5	6	7	8	9	10	11
Top	29¾	29¾	26⅞	25⅜	24	22½	21⅛	19⅝	18¼	16¾	16¾
Bottom	31¼	29¾	28⅜	26⅞	26⅞	28⅜	16¾	15⅜	13⅞	12¾	11
Column #	12	13	14	15	16	17	18	19	20	21	22
Top	22½	9½	8⅛	6⅝	5¼	5¼	13⅞	12⅜	11	11	12⅜
Bottom	11	12⅜	13⅞	5¼	5¼	6⅝	8⅛	9½	22½	19⅝	18¼
Column #	23	24	25	26	27	28	29	30	31		
Top	13⅞	15⅜	16¾	28⅜	26⅞	26⅞	28⅜	29¾	31¼		
Bottom	18¼	19⅝	21⅛	22½	24	25⅜	26⅞	29¾	29¾		

Construction

See Making a 3-D Quilt (page 7) for complete instructions on sewing the columns of triangles and assembling the quilt.

SEW THE COLUMNS

1. For column 1 in the 66½″ × 84″ quilt, start with a 2½″ background strip that is 24″ long with a 60° left-leaning angle at the bottom. To continue the first column, *add triangles in this order:*

1 light orange triangle	1 background
8 dark orange	1 light blue
7 background	2 dark blue
1 light orange	1 strip 2½″ × 25⅛″ with a 60° right-leaning angle at the top
10 dark orange	

For column 1 in the 83″ × 105″ quilt, start with a 3″ background strip that is 29¾″ long with a 60° left-leaning angle at the bottom. To continue the first column, *add triangles in this order:*

1 light orange triangle	1 background
8 dark orange	1 light blue
7 background	2 dark blue
1 light orange	1 strip 3″ × 31¼″ with a 60° right-leaning angle at the top
10 dark orange	

2. Follow the *Hygge* design chart (page 43) and continue to build the remaining columns in the same manner.

QUILT ASSEMBLY

1. Sew the columns together.

2. Trim the top and bottom of the quilt to square as described in Trimming to Square (page 10).

BORDERS

See Adding Borders (page 10). Before you cut the borders, measure your pieced quilt top and adjust the following sizes to match your quilt.

1. For the 66½″ × 84″ quilt, make 2 side borders 2½″ × 80″ and top and bottom borders 2½″ × 66½″.

For the 83″ × 105″ quilt, make 2 side borders 3″ × 100½″ and top and bottom borders 3″ × 83″.

2. Add the side borders to the quilt, then add the top and bottom borders.

*alternate
color inspiration*

 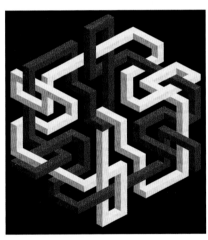 

1 2 3 4 5 6 7 8 9 10 11 12 13 14 15 16 17 18 19 20 21 22 23 24 25 26 27 28 29 30 31

Hygge Design Chart

Whale's Tail

Finished quilt sizes:
60½˝ × 77½˝ and 84½˝ × 108½˝

Whale's Tail gets its name from its similarity to the appearance of the tail end of a breaching whale.

Draw It

Refer to Drawing Horizontal Diamonds (page 13) and Drawing Left- and Right-Facing Vertical Diamonds (page 14) to see the building blocks for the *Whale's Tail* drawing.

1. Start with a 10-block left facing diamond. **A**

2. Attach a 10-block right facing diamond. **B**

3. Attach a 10-block horizontal diamond. **C**

4. Add 5 more triple diamond units. **D**

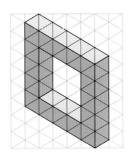

A

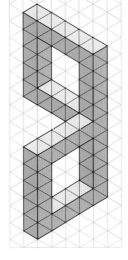

B

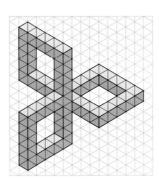

C

D

Materials and Cutting

Start by cutting the number of strips in the width required for your quilt, then cut the strips into triangles (page 8).

	YARDAGE REQUIREMENTS, WIDTH OF STRIPS, NUMBER OF STRIPS TO CUT				
Fabrics	**60½″ × 77½″ quilt, cut 3″ strips**		**84½″ × 108½″ quilt, cut 4″ strips**		**Triangles to cut from strips**
	Yardage	3″ strips to cut	Yardage	4″ strips to cut	
Light Purple	½ yard	5	1 yard	7	82
Medium Purple	½ yard	5	1 yard	7	82
Dark Purple	½ yard	5	1 yard	7	82
Light Blue	½ yard	5	1 yard	7	82
Medium Blue	½ yard	5	1 yard	7	82
Dark Blue	½ yard	5	1 yard	7	82
Light Yellow	½ yard	5	1 yard	7	82
Medium Yellow	½ yard	5	1 yard	7	82
Dark Orange	½ yard	5	1 yard	7	82
Background	2 yards	22	3⅝ yards	30	384
Border	¾ yard	8	1⅓ yards	11	
Backing	4¾ yards		7¾ yards		
Binding	⅝ yard		⅞ yard		
Batting	69″ × 84″		93″ × 117″		

Construction

See Making a 3-D Quilt (page 7) for complete instructions on sewing the columns of triangles and assembling the quilt.

SEW THE COLUMNS

1. For column 1, start with a background triangle with the blunt point oriented towards the right, then add the next background triangle with the blunt point facing to the left.

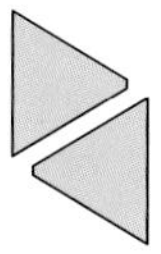

To continue the first column, *add triangles in this order:*

9 more background triangles

1 light purple

2 dark purple

1 background

1 light yellow

8 dark orange

3 background

1 light yellow

8 dark orange

1 background

1 light blue

2 dark blue

11 background

2. For column 2, start with a background triangle with the blunt point oriented towards the left, then add the next background triangle with the blunt point facing to the right.

To continue the second column, *add triangles in this order:*

8 more background triangles	2 dark orange
3 light purple	1 background
2 dark purple	2 light yellow
2 light yellow	8 medium yellow
2 dark orange	3 light blue
3 medium yellow	2 dark blue
1 light yellow	10 background

3. Follow the *Whale's Tail* design chart (page 47) and continue to build columns 3–22 in the same manner.

QUILT ASSEMBLY

1. Sew the columns together.

2. Trim the top and bottom of the quilt to square as described in Trimming to Square (page 10).

BORDERS

See Adding Borders (page 10). Before you cut the borders, measure your pieced quilt top and adjust the following sizes to match your quilt.

1. For the 60½˝ × 77½˝ quilt, make 2 side borders 3˝ × 72½˝ and top and bottom borders 3˝ × 60½˝.

For the 84½˝ × 108½˝ quilt, make 2 side borders 4˝ × 101½˝ and top and bottom borders 4˝ × 84½˝.

2. Add the side borders to the quilt, then add the top and bottom borders.

alternate color inspiration

Whale's Tail Design Chart

Huckleberry

Finished quilt sizes:
40½˝ × 46˝ and 56½˝ × 64˝

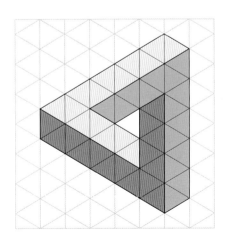

I had originally drawn *Huckleberry* with all blue triangles and a green background, which to me gave it the look of the wild blueberries in the woods behind my northern Michigan home.

Draw It

Refer to Drawing "Impossible" Triangles (page 15) to see the building blocks for the *Huckleberry* drawing.

1. Start with a 10-block Impossible Triangle. **A**

2. Add a second mirror image 10-block Impossible Triangle. **B**

3. Continue to add triangles to form a large hexagon. **C**

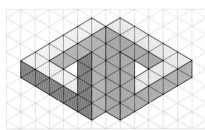

A

B

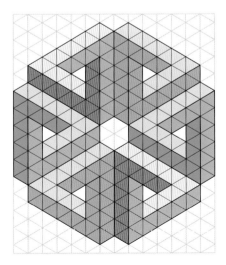

C

Materials and Cutting

Start by cutting the number of strips in the width required for your quilt, then cut the strips into triangles (page 8).

Fabrics	40½˝ × 46˝ quilt, cut 3˝ strips		56½˝ × 64˝ quilt, cut 4˝ strips		Triangles to cut from strips
	Yardage	3˝ strips to cut	Yardage	4˝ strips to cut	
Light Blue	¼ yard	2	½ yard	3	30
Medium Blue	¼ yard	2	½ yard	3	30
Dark Blue	¼ yard	2	½ yard	3	30
Light Pink	¼ yard	2	½ yard	3	30
Medium Pink	¼ yard	2	½ yard	3	30
Dark Pink	¼ yard	2	½ yard	3	30
Light Green	¼ yard	2	½ yard	3	30
Medium Green	¼ yard	2	½ yard	3	30
Dark Green	¼ yard	2	½ yard	3	30
Background	¾ yard	8	1½ yards	11	136
Border	½ yard	5	1 yard	7	
Backing	2¾ yards		3¾ yards		
Binding	½ yard		⅝ yard		
Batting	49˝ × 54˝		65˝ × 72˝		

Table header: **YARDAGE REQUIREMENTS, WIDTH OF STRIPS, NUMBER OF STRIPS TO CUT**

Construction

See Making a 3-D Quilt (page 7) for complete instructions on sewing the columns of triangles and assembling the quilt.

SEW THE COLUMNS

1. For column 1, start with a background triangle with the blunt point oriented towards the right, then add the next background triangle with the blunt point facing to the left.

To continue the first column, *add triangles in this order:*

- 7 more background triangles
- 1 light green
- 10 dark green
- 9 background

2. For column 2, start with a background triangle with the blunt point oriented towards the left, then add the next background triangle with the blunt point facing to the right.

To continue the second column, *add triangles in this order:*

- 4 more background triangles
- 1 light pink
- 2 dark pink
- 2 light green

- 2 dark green
- 7 medium green
- 1 light blue
- 2 dark blue
- 6 background

3. Follow the *Huckleberry* design chart (page 51) and continue to build columns 3–14 in the same manner.

QUILT ASSEMBLY

1. Sew the columns together.

2. Trim the top and bottom of the quilt to square as described in Trimming to Square (page 10).

BORDERS

See Adding Borders (page 10). Before you cut the borders, measure your pieced quilt top and adjust the following sizes to match your quilt.

1. For the 40½˝ × 46˝ quilt, make 2 side borders 3˝ × 41˝ and top and bottom borders 3˝ × 40½˝.

For the 56½˝ × 64˝ quilt, make 2 side borders 4˝ × 57˝ and top and bottom borders 4˝ × 56½˝.

2. Add the side borders to the quilt, then add the top and bottom borders.

alternate color inspiration

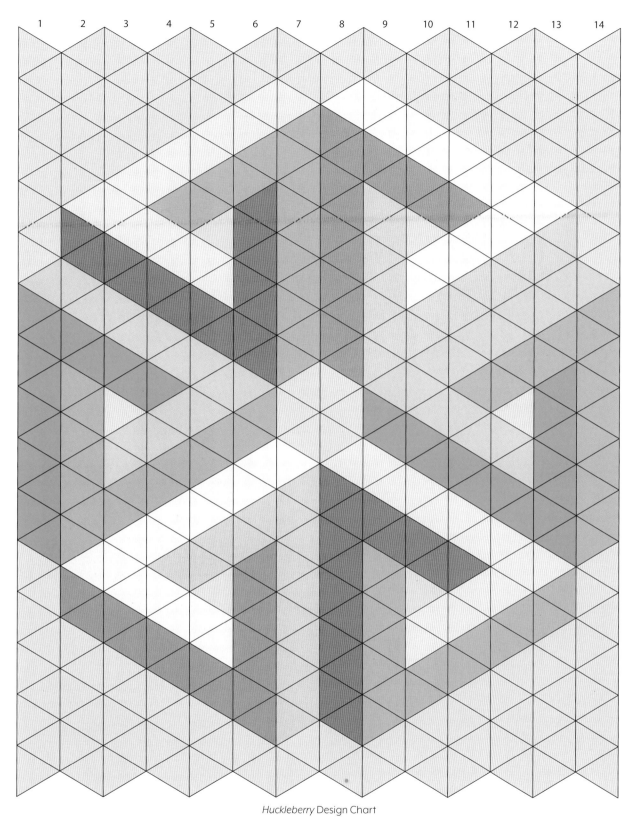

Huckleberry Design Chart

Shenanigans

The *Shenanigans* drawing started with the green center which reminded me of a fidget spinner toy that was all the rage a few years ago. The object of a fidget spinner was to keep the hands of the spinner busy enough to avoid other shenanigans.

Draw It

Refer to Drawing Horizontal Diamonds (page 13), Drawing Left- and Right-Facing Vertical Diamonds (page 14), and Drawing Crisscrossing 3-D Beams (page 14) to see the building blocks for the *Shenanigans* drawing.

1. Draw 5 connected 10-block horizontal diamonds. **A**

2. Add 3 sets of connected 10-block vertical left-facing diamonds. **B**

3. Add interwoven connecting beams. **C**

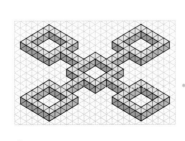

A

B

C

Materials and Cutting

Start by cutting the number of strips in the width required for your quilt, then cut the strips into triangles (page 8).

	YARDAGE REQUIREMENTS, WIDTH OF STRIPS, NUMBER OF STRIPS TO CUT				
Fabrics	**56½˝ × 76˝ quilt, cut 2½˝ strips**		**70½˝ × 95˝ quilt, cut 3˝ strips**		**Triangles to cut from strips**
	Yardage	**2½˝ strips to cut**	**Yardage**	**3˝ strips to cut**	
Light Green	¾ yard	8	1 yard	10	164
Medium Green	⅓ yard	4	½ yard	4	69
Dark Green	⅓ yard	4	½ yard	4	69
Light Yellow	⅓ yard	4	½ yard	4	69
Medium Yellow	⅔ yard	8	1 yard	9	151
Dark Yellow	1 yard	12	1¼ yards	14	246
Light Aqua	⅓ yard	4	½ yard	5	84
Medium Aqua	½ yard	6	¾ yard	6	106
Dark Aqua	½ yard	5	¾ yard	6	91
Background	2¼ yards	29	3 yards	33	589
Border	⅝ yard	7	⅞ yard	9	
Backing	4¾ yards		5⅞ yards		
Binding	⅝ yard		⅞ yard		
Batting	65˝ × 84˝		79˝ × 103˝		

Construction

See Making a 3-D Quilt (page 7) for complete instructions on sewing the columns of triangles and assembling the quilt.

SEW THE COLUMNS

1. For column 1, start with a background triangle with the blunt point oriented towards the right, then add the next background triangle with the blunt point facing to the left.

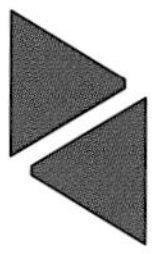

To continue the first column, *add triangles in this order:*

9 more background triangles

1 light aqua

9 dark aqua

1 light green

2 dark green

6 dark aqua

1 background

1 light aqua

5 dark aqua

1 light green

2 dark green

14 dark aqua

9 background

2. For column 2, start with a background triangle with the blunt point oriented towards the left, then add the next background triangle with the blunt point facing to the right.

To continue the second column, *add triangles in this order:*

8 more background triangles	2 light aqua
2 light aqua	4 medium aqua
8 medium aqua	3 light green
3 light green	2 dark green
2 dark green	11 medium aqua
3 medium aqua	1 light aqua
1 light aqua	2 dark aqua
1 dark aqua	8 background

3. Follow the *Shenanigans* design chart (page 55) and continue to build columns 3–26 in the same manner.

QUILT ASSEMBLY

1. Sew the columns together.

2. Trim the top and bottom of the quilt to square as described in Trimming to Square (page 10).

BORDERS

See Adding Borders (page 10). Before you cut the borders, measure your pieced quilt top and adjust the following sizes to match your quilt.

1. For the 56½˝ × 76˝ quilt, make 2 side borders 2½˝ × 72˝ and top and bottom borders 2½˝ × 56½˝.

For the 70½˝ × 95˝ quilt, make 2 side borders 3˝ × 90˝ and top and bottom borders 3˝ × 70½˝.

2. Add the side borders to the quilt, then add the top and bottom borders.

alternate color inspiration

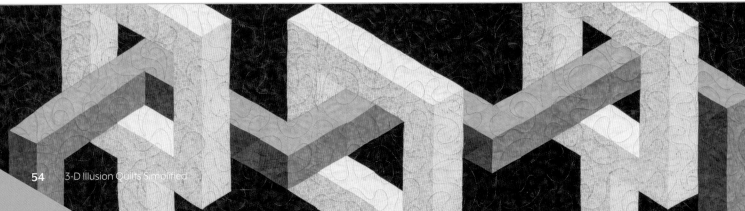

Shenanigans Design Chart

Limerick

From Wikipedia: "A limerick is a form of verse, usually humorous and frequently rude, in five-line, trimeter with a strict rhyme scheme of AABBA, in which the first, second, and fifth lines rhyme, while the third and fourth lines are shorter and share a different rhyme." The *Limerick* drawing is built top to bottom like a limerick, with rhyming top and bottom and narrower (shorter) middle section.

Draw It

Refer to Drawing Horizontal Diamonds (page 13) to see the building blocks for the *Limerick* drawing.

1. Draw 2 overlapping 20-block horizontal diamonds. **A**

2. Add 2 additional interlocked 20-block horizontal diamonds. **B**

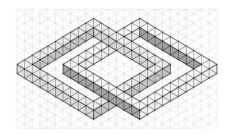

A

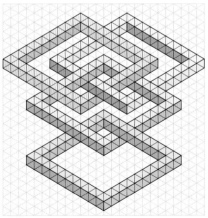

B

3. Add another set of overlapping 20-block horizontal diamonds. **C**

4. Add two 8-block horizontal diamonds. **D**

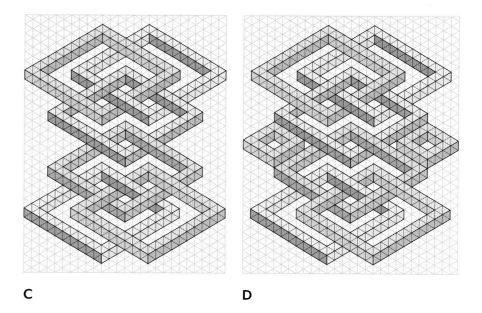

C   D

Materials and Cutting

Start by cutting the number of strips in the width required for your quilt, then cut the strips into triangles (page 8).

	YARDAGE REQUIREMENTS, WIDTH OF STRIPS, NUMBER OF STRIPS TO CUT				
Fabrics	75½˝ × 83½˝ quilt, cut 3˝ strips		90½˝ × 100˝ quilt, cut 3½˝ strips		**Triangles to cut from strips**
	Yardage	**3˝ strips to cut**	**Yardage**	**3½˝ strips to cut**	
Light Green	½ yard	4	⅝ yard	4	60
Medium Green	¼ yard	2	⅓ yard	2	27
Dark Blue	¼ yard	2	½ yard	3	31
Light Yellow	½ yard	4	⅝ yard	4	60
Medium Yellow	¼ yard	2	⅓ yard	2	27
Orange	¼ yard	2	½ yard	3	31
Light Pink	1 yard	11	1⅝ yards	13	184
Medium Pink	½ yard	5	⅞ yard	6	84
Periwinkle	⅔ yard	6	⅞ yard	7	92
Beige	⅔ yard	7	1 yard	8	120
Medium Aqua	⅓ yard	3	⅝ yard	4	54
Dark Aqua	½ yard	4	⅔ yard	5	62
Background	3 yards	34	4¾ yards	41	604
Pieced inner border	⅓ yard	4	¾	6	
Border	⅞ yard	9	1⅛	10	
Backing	7 yards		8¼ yards		
Binding	¾ yard		⅞ yard		
Batting	84˝ × 92˝		99˝ × 108˝		

Construction

See Making a 3-D Quilt (page 7) for complete instructions on sewing the columns of triangles and assembling the quilt.

SEW THE COLUMNS

1. For column 1, start with a background triangle with the blunt point oriented towards the right, then add the next background triangle with the blunt point facing to the left.

To continue the first column, *add triangles in this order:*

9 more background triangles	2 periwinkle
1 light pink	11 background
2 periwinkle	1 beige
11 background	2 dark aqua
3 light pink	11 background

2. For column 2, start with a background triangle with the blunt point oriented towards the left, then add the next background triangle with the blunt point facing to the right.

To continue the second column, *add triangles in this order:*

8 more background triangles	2 light pink
3 light pink	2 periwinkle
2 periwinkle	9 background
9 background	3 beige
2 light pink	2 dark aqua
1 medium pink	10 background

3. Follow the *Limerick* design chart (page 60) and continue to build columns 3–26 in the same manner.

PREPARING THE PRE-BORDERS

The pre-borders are columns A and B on the *Limerick* design chart.

1. To create a left pre-border for the 75½″ × 83½″ quilt, cut and piece 2 background strips 3″ × 42″.

2. For each, cut one end cut at 60° as shown in the diagram.

3. Start with the top long background piece, add 1 light pink triangle, 2 periwinkle triangles, and the second long piece. (You will trim the borders as necessary in Quilt Assembly, page 60.)

4. To create a right pre-border for the 75½″ × 83½″ quilt, cut and piece 2 background strips 3″ × 42″.

5. For each, cut one end cut at 60° as shown in the diagram.

6. Start with the top background piece, add 1 light pink triangle, 2 medium pink triangles, and the second long piece. (You will trim the borders as necessary in Quilt Assembly, page 10.)

For the 90½″ × 100″ quilt, cut and piece 4 background strips 3½″ × 50″ and follow Steps 2, 3, 5, and 6 above.

QUILT ASSEMBLY

1. Sew the columns together.

2. Match the triangles in the right and left borders to the triangles in the quilt top and attach them to the sides of the quilt. Leave the background strips long to trim to square with the rest of the quilt top.

3. Trim the top and bottom of the quilt to square as described in Trimming to Square (page 10).

BORDERS

See Adding Borders (page 10). Before you cut the borders, measure your pieced quilt top and adjust the following sizes to match your quilt.

1. For the 75½″ × 83½″ quilt, make 2 side borders 3″ × 78½″ and top and bottom borders 3″ × 75½″.

For the 90½″ × 100″ quilt, make 2 side borders 3½″ × 94″ and top and bottom borders 3½″ × 90½″.

2. Add the side borders to the quilt, then add the top and bottom borders.

Limerick Design Chart

Arpeggio

Finished quilt sizes:
55½″ × 80½″ and 77½″ × 112½″

Arpeggio is named after a pleasing musical construct.

Draw It

Refer to Drawing "Impossible" Triangles (page 15) to see the building blocks for the *Arpeggio* drawing.

1. Start with a 16-block Impossible Triangle. **A**

2. Add 5 additional Impossible Triangles to form a large hexagon. **B**

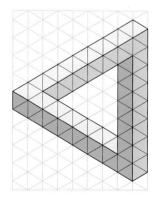

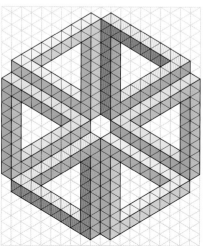

A   B

3. Weave a connecting beam in and out of the triangles. **C**

4. Add four 14-block Impossible Triangles. **D**

5. Finish with a connecting beam. **E**

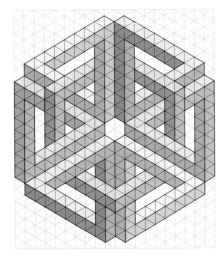

C

D

E

Materials and Cutting

Start by cutting the number of strips in the width required for your quilt, then cut the strips into triangles (page 8).

	YARDAGE REQUIREMENTS, WIDTH OF STRIPS, NUMBER OF STRIPS TO CUT					
Fabrics	**55½˝ × 80½˝ quilt, cut 3˝ strips**		**77½˝ × 112½˝ quilt, cut 4˝ strips**		**Triangles to cut from strips**
	Yardage	**3˝ strips to cut**	**Yardage**	**4˝ strips to cut**	
Light Green	¾ yard	8	1¼ yards	10	128
Medium Green	⅔ yard	7	1⅛ yards	9	111
Dark Green	⅔ yard	7	1⅛ yards	9	111
Light Orange	½ yard	5	1 yard	7	88
Medium Orange	½ yard	4	1 yard	6	72
Dark Orange	½ yard	4	1 yard	6	72
Light Aqua	⅓ yard	3	⅝ yard	4	42
Medium Aqua	⅓ yard	3	⅝ yard	4	42
Dark Aqua	⅓ yard	3	⅝ yard	4	46
Light Purple	⅓ yard	3	⅝ yard	4	42
Medium Purple	⅓ yard	3	⅝ yard	4	46
Dark Purple	⅓ yard	3	⅝ yard	4	42
Background	1¼ yards	13	2⅛ yards	17	218
Border	¾ yard	7	1¼ yards	10	
Backing	5 yards		7¼ yards		
Binding	⅝ yard		⅞ yard		
Batting	64˝ × 89˝		86˝ × 121˝		

Construction

See Making a 3-D Quilt (page 7) for complete instructions on sewing the columns of triangles and assembling the quilt.

SEW THE COLUMNS

1. For column 1, start with a background triangle with the blunt point oriented towards the left, then add the next background triangle with the blunt point facing to the right.

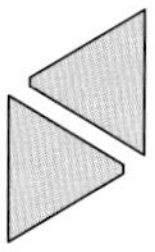

To continue the first column, *add triangles in this order:*

6 more background triangles

1 light green

2 dark green

1 background

1 light orange

5 dark orange

1 light green

16 dark green

6 dark orange

1 background

1 light green

2 dark green

8 background

2. For column 2, start with a background triangle with the blunt point oriented towards the right, then add the next background triangle with the blunt point facing to the left.

To continue the second column, *add triangles in this order:*

5 more background triangles	13 medium green
3 light green	1 light purple
2 dark green	2 dark purple
1 light orange	1 medium orange
2 medium orange	1 light orange
1 light aqua	1 dark orange
2 dark aqua	3 light green
2 light green	2 dark green
2 dark green	7 background

3. Follow the *Arpeggio* design chart (page 65) and continue to build columns 3–20 in the same manner.

QUILT ASSEMBLY

1. Sew the columns together.

2. Trim the top and bottom of the quilt to square as described in Trimming to Square (page 10).

BORDERS

See Adding Borders (page 10). Before you cut the borders, measure your pieced quilt top and adjust the following sizes to match your quilt.

1. For the 55½˝ × 80½˝ quilt, make 2 side borders 3˝ × 75½˝ and top and bottom borders 3˝ × 55½˝.

For the 77½˝ × 112½˝ quilt, make 2 side borders 4˝ × 105½˝ and top and bottom borders 4˝ × 77½˝.

2. Add the side borders to the quilt, then add the top and bottom borders.

alternate color inspiration

1 2 3 4 5 6 7 8 9 10 11 12 13 14 15 16 17 18 19 20

Arpeggio Design Chart

Better Together
Bed Runner

Finished quilt sizes: 70½˝ × 29½˝ and 88˝ × 36½˝

The idea behind the *Better Together Bed Runner* was that it could be used as a "welcome" decoration across the foot of a bed in a guest bedroom or as a table runner for a holiday family dinner.

Draw It

Refer to Drawing Simple Shapes on Isometric Paper; Hearts and Stars (page 15) to see the building blocks for the *Better Together Bed Runner* drawing.

1. Draw a 3-D Heart. **A**

2. Add a connecting heart, erasing the portion you would like to appear behind. **B**

3. Continue to add connecting hearts. **C**

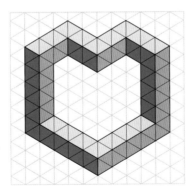

A

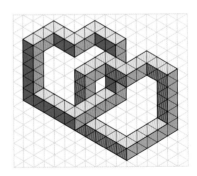

B

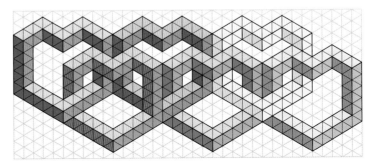

C

Materials and Cutting

Start by cutting the number of strips in the width required for your quilt, then cut the strips into triangles (page 8).

	YARDAGE REQUIREMENTS, WIDTH OF STRIPS, NUMBER OF STRIPS TO CUT				
Fabrics	**70½″ × 29½″ quilt, cut 2½″ strips**		**88″ × 36½″ quilt, cut 3″ strips**		**Triangles to cut from strips**
	Yardage	2½″ strips to cut	Yardage	3″ strips to cut	
Light Blue	¼ yard	2	¼ yard	2	32
Medium Blue	¼ yard	2	¼ yard	2	28
Dark Blue	¼ yard	2	¼ yard	2	28
Light Pink	¼ yard	2	¼ yard	2	32
Medium Pink	¼ yard	2	¼ yard	2	28
Dark Pink	¼ yard	2	¼ yard	2	28
Light Purple	¼ yard	2	¼ yard	2	28
Medium Purple	¼ yard	1	¼ yard	2	24
Dark Purple	¼ yard	1	¼ yard	1	20
Light Green	¼ yard	2	¼ yard	2	32
Medium Green	¼ yard	1	¼ yard	2	24
Dark Green	¼ yard	1	¼ yard	2	24
Light Yellow	¼ yard	2	¼ yard	2	32
Medium Yellow	¼ yard	1	¼ yard	2	24
Dark Yellow	¼ yard	1	¼ yard	2	24
Light Aqua	¼ yard	2	¼ yard	2	32
Medium Aqua	¼ yard	2	¼ yard	2	28
Dark Aqua	¼ yard	2	¼ yard	2	28
Background	1¼ yards	16	1⅝ yards	19	414
Backing	2¼ yards		2¾ yards		
Binding	½ yard		⅝ yard		
Batting	74″ × 33″		92″ × 40″		

Construction

See Making a 3-D Quilt (page 7) for complete instructions on sewing the columns of triangles and assembling the quilt.

SEW THE COLUMNS

1. For column 1, start with a background triangle with the blunt point oriented towards the left, then add the next background triangle with the blunt point facing to the right.

To continue the first column, *add triangles in this order:*

> 2 more background triangles
>
> 1 light blue
>
> 10 dark blue
>
> 11 background

2. For column 2, start with a background triangle with the blunt point oriented towards the right, then add the next background triangle with the blunt point facing to the left.

To continue the second column, *add triangles in this order:*

> 1 more background triangles
>
> 2 light blue
>
> 8 medium blue
>
> 1 light blue
>
> 2 dark blue
>
> 10 background

3. Follow the *Better Together Bed Runner* design chart (below) and continue to build columns 3–35 in the same manner.

QUILT ASSEMBLY

1. Sew the columns together.

2. Trim the top and bottom of the quilt to square as described in Trimming to Square (page 10).

alternate color inspiration

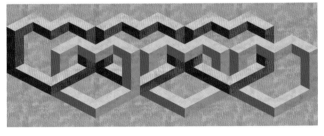

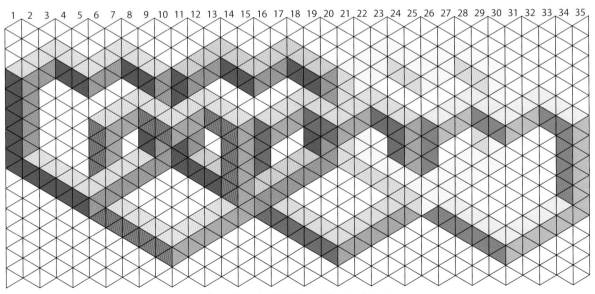

Better Together Bed Runner Design Chart

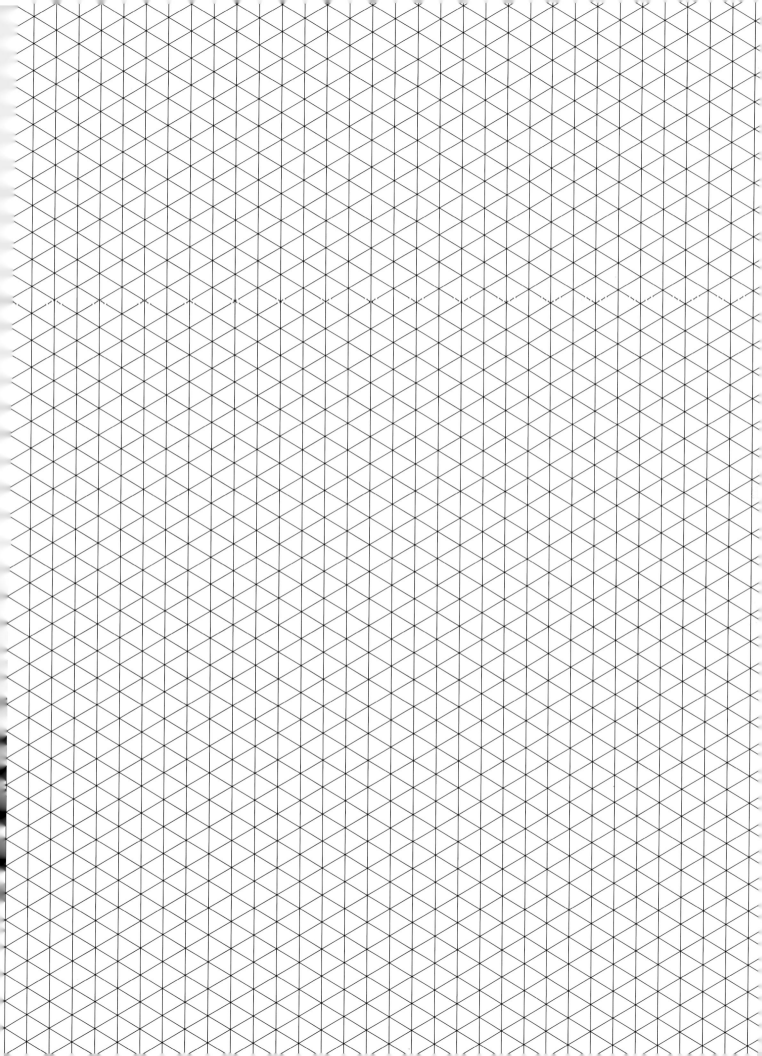

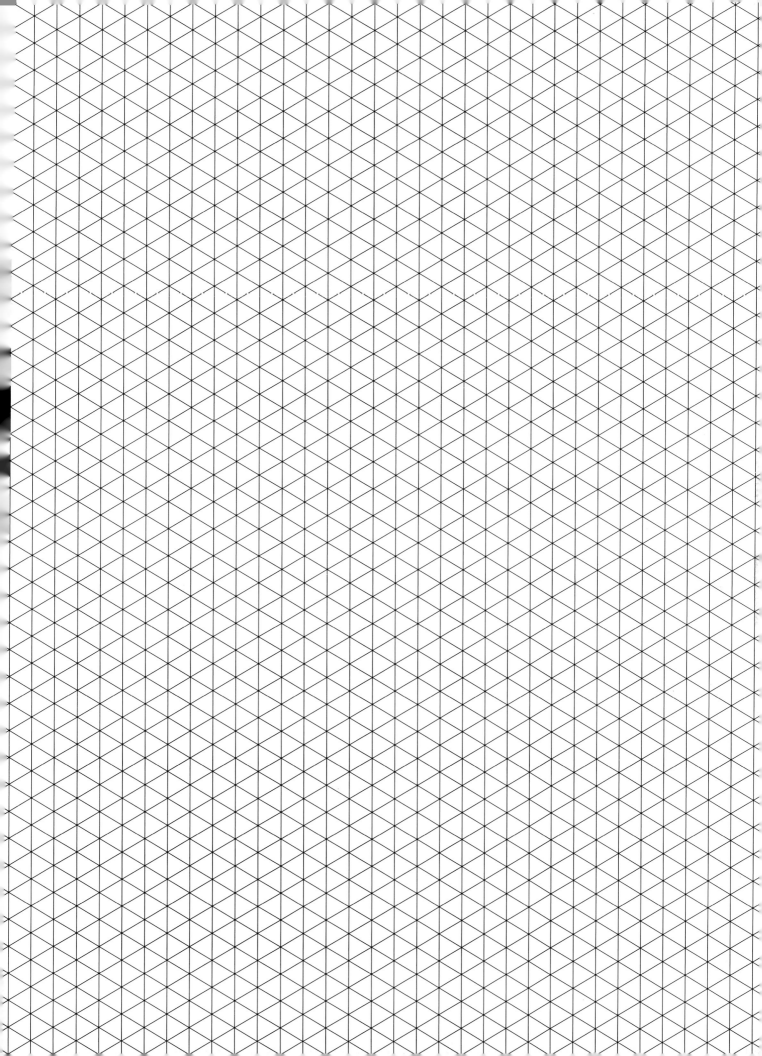

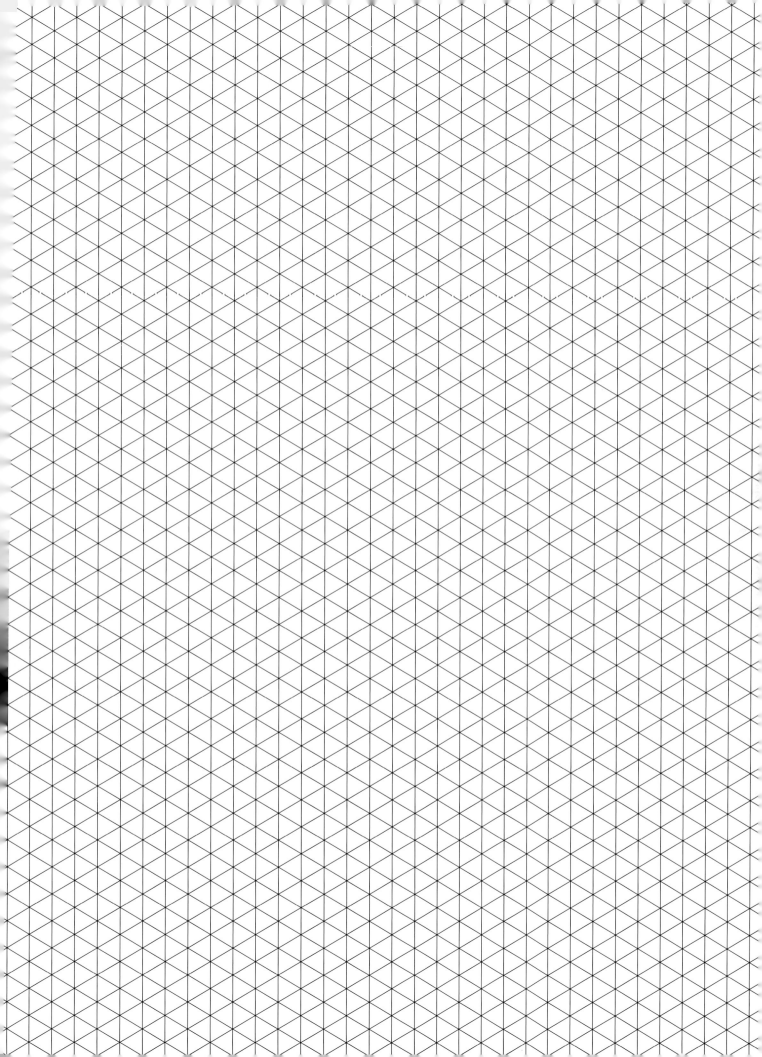

About the Author

Ruth Ann Berry lives in rural northern Michigan where she owns a small town quilt shop and online business. She writes books and patterns with an emphasis on geometric design and bright color. She travels extensively to exhibit and teach at quilt festivals and guilds. She looks forward to retiring from full-time pharmacy work to focus on quilt design, gardens, and grandchildren.

Visit Ruth Ann online and follow on social media!

Website: quiltersclinic.com

Facebook: The Quilter's Clinic

ALSO BY
Ruth Ann Berry

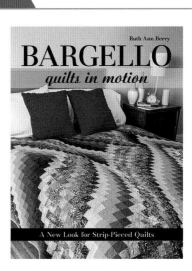

CREATIVE SPARK

ONLINE LEARNING

Quilting courses to become an expert quilter...

From their studio to yours, Creative Spark instructors are teaching you how to create and become a master of your craft. So not only do you get a look inside their creative space, you also get to be a part of engaging courses that would typically be a one or multi-day workshop from the comfort of your home.

Creative Spark is not your one-size-fits-all online learning experience. We welcome you to be who you are, share, create, and belong.

Scan for a gift from us!

creativespark.ctpub.com